Table Of Contents

Chapter 2: Challenges Faced by Older Workers and Displaced Employees 1
Chapter 3: Benefits of Natural Language Processing for Older Workers 1
Chapter 4: NLP Tools and Technologies for Career Pivoting............1
Chapter 5: Success Stories of Older Workers Using NLP 1
Chapter 6: Overcoming Barriers and Embracing Change 1
Chapter 7: Future Trends and Opportunities in NLP for Older Workers 1
Chapter 8: Conclusion and Call to Action...1
Chapter 1: Understanding Natural Language Processing...................1

Chapter 1: Understanding Natural Language Processing

What is Natural Language Processing (NLP)?

Natural Language Processing (NLP) is a field of artificial intelligence that focuses on the interaction between computers and humans using natural language. In simpler terms, NLP allows computers to understand, interpret, and generate human language. This technology has a wide range of applications, from virtual assistants like Siri and Alexa to language translation services and sentiment analysis tools.

For older workforce employees and displaced workers, NLP offers a unique opportunity to leverage their experience and skills in a rapidly evolving digital landscape. Unlike other emerging technologies that may require extensive technical knowledge or coding skills, NLP can be easily adopted by individuals with a background in communication, customer service, or other fields that require strong language skills. This makes NLP an ideal tool for older workers looking to stay relevant in today's job market.

One of the key benefits of NLP for older or displaced employees is its ability to automate repetitive tasks and streamline workflows. By utilizing NLP-powered chatbots or virtual assistants, employees can offload mundane tasks like answering customer inquiries or scheduling appointments, allowing them to focus on more strategic and value-added activities. This not only increases productivity but also reduces the risk of burnout and job dissatisfaction among employees.

For displaced workers looking to pivot their careers, NLP can be a game-changer. With the right training and resources, individuals can quickly upskill and transition into roles that leverage NLP technology. Whether it's working as a data analyst, content strategist, or UX designer, NLP skills are in high demand across various industries, making it a viable option for those looking to make a career change.

In conclusion, Natural Language Processing (NLP) is a powerful tool that can benefit older workforce employees and displaced workers in numerous ways. From automating tasks to opening up new career opportunities, NLP has the potential to empower individuals to thrive in today's digital economy. By embracing this technology and investing in the necessary training, older workers can stay competitive in the job market and displaced employees can pivot their careers with confidence.

History of NLP

The history of Natural Language Processing (NLP) dates back to the 1950s, when researchers began exploring ways to enable computers to understand and process human language. Over the decades, significant advancements have been made in NLP, leading to its widespread use in various applications such as virtual assistants, chatbots, and language translation tools. Older workforce employees and displaced workers can benefit greatly from the evolution of

NLP technology, as it offers new opportunities for career growth and skills development.

One of the reasons why NLP is perfect for older or displaced employees is its ability to enhance communication and productivity in the workplace. By leveraging NLP tools and techniques, older workers can improve their efficiency in tasks such as writing emails, analyzing data, and conducting research. This can help them stay competitive in the job market and adapt to the changing demands of the digital age. Additionally, NLP can assist displaced employees in transitioning to new careers by providing them with the necessary skills and knowledge to succeed in emerging fields such as data science, artificial intelligence, and machine learning.

For displaced employees looking to pivot their careers, NLP offers a range of opportunities for upskilling and reskilling. By learning how to use NLP tools and technologies, displaced workers can acquire valuable skills that are in high demand in today's job market. This can open up new career paths and enable them to pursue roles in industries such as healthcare, finance, and marketing. With the right training and guidance, displaced employees can leverage NLP to reinvent themselves and thrive in the digital economy.

As NLP continues to evolve and advance, older workforce employees and displaced workers have the opportunity to benefit from its transformative capabilities. By embracing NLP technology and incorporating it into their daily work routines, older workers can enhance their communication skills, boost their productivity, and stay relevant in their respective industries. Displaced employees, on the other hand, can use NLP as a steppingstone to pivot their careers and explore new opportunities in emerging fields. This is exactly what I did. I learned a skillset that kept me relevant! With the right mindset and willingness to learn, older and displaced workers can empower themselves with NLP and take their professional development to new heights.

In conclusion, the history of NLP is a testament to the power of innovation and technology in transforming the way we communicate and interact with machines. For older employees and displaced workers, NLP offers a gateway to new possibilities and career advancement. By embracing NLP and harnessing its potential, older and displaced employees can equip themselves with the skills and knowledge needed to thrive in the digital age. With the right support and resources, they can leverage NLP to empower themselves and build a successful and fulfilling career.

Applications of NLP in the workplace

Natural Language Processing (NLP) is a powerful tool that can benefit displaced workers in the workplace in various ways. One of the key applications of NLP in the workplace is in improving communication and collaboration among team members. Older workers often bring years of experience and knowledge to the table, and NLP can help them share their insights more effectively with their colleagues. By using NLP tools such as chatbots and sentiment analysis, older workers can communicate more efficiently and work together more seamlessly.

Another important application of NLP in the workplace is in enhancing productivity and efficiency. Older workers may struggle with keeping up with the latest technological advancements, but NLP bridges that gap by automating routine tasks and providing real-time insights. By using NLP tools to analyze data and make predictions, older workers can make more informed decisions and improve their overall performance.

For displaced workers looking to pivot their careers, NLP can be a valuable tool in helping them transition into new roles or industries. NLP technology can help displaced workers identify their transferable skills and strengths, as well as explore new career opportunities that align with their interests and goals. By leveraging NLP tools such as resume parsers and job matching algorithms, displaced workers can streamline their job search process and find new employment opportunities more quickly and efficiently. Based on my experience, I would suggest that you learn the development aspect of NLP. I found that I am only limited to my imagination. Critical thinking and proper "prompting" will take you a long way. Spend the money on classes by Udemy or some other organization. Courses are really inexpensive based on the learned skill set.

Furthermore, NLP can also help older or displaced employees enhance their learning and development opportunities. By using NLP-powered language learning tools or virtual assistants, older workers can improve their skills and knowledge in a more personalized and interactive way. NLP can help older workers stay relevant in the ever-changing job market and adapt to new technologies and trends.

In conclusion, the applications of NLP in the workplace are vast and varied, making it a perfect tool for older or displaced employees looking to enhance their skills, productivity, and career opportunities. By embracing NLP technology, older workers can leverage their experience and expertise to thrive in the modern workplace, while displaced workers can pivot their careers and find new paths to success. I was at a crossroads. My position as Facility Manager was eliminated when I was 58 years old. I was now faced with the task of locating a position that paid enough to help pay the bills. My wife and I struggled over the next two years. I was constantly sending out resumes while honing my NLP skills. Today I have developed over 100 NLP Applications. I feel there are probably 20 that are home runs. As my wife and I prepare to launch three websites that will market these applications, the anticipation level is high as are our hopes. We know that God is in control of all of it. For those of you that do not believe, I do not judge. I think about the alternative. I choose to believe. Fully.

Chapter 2: Challenges Faced by Older Workers and Displaced Employees

Ageism in the Workplace

Ageism in the workplace is a pervasive issue that older workforce employees and displaced workers face regularly. No, age discrimination is not legal, but it happens daily! This form of discrimination is based on negative stereotypes and assumptions about older individuals' capabilities and productivity. Many older workers are overlooked for job opportunities or promotions simply because of their age, despite having the skills and experience necessary for the role. This can be demoralizing and lead to feelings of inadequacy and frustration among older employees. Do not subscribe to this. You have experiences that can translate into valuable skills in the world of NLP.
Natural Language Processing (NLP) is a technology that holds great potential for older or displaced employees looking to remain competitive in the workforce. NLP uses algorithms to analyze and understand human language, making it an ideal tool for processing large amounts of textual data quickly and efficiently. Older workers who may not have the technical skills of their younger counterparts can benefit from NLP's user-friendly interface and intuitive design. This technology can help older workers enhance their productivity and efficiency in the workplace, ultimately combating ageism and proving their value to employers.
For displaced employees looking to pivot their careers, NLP can be a valuable asset in navigating the job market and identifying new opportunities. By leveraging NLP tools to analyze job postings and industry trends, displaced workers can gain insights into in-demand skills and qualifications. This information can help them tailor their resumes and cover letters to better align with the needs of potential employers, increasing their chances of landing a new job. Additionally, NLP can assist displaced workers in identifying transferable skills from their previous roles and highlighting them to prospective employers in a compelling way.
One of the key benefits of NLP for older or displaced employees is its ability to level the playing field in the job market. By automating repetitive tasks and providing actionable insights, NLP can help older workers maintain their productivity and competitiveness alongside younger colleagues. This can help dispel ageist stereotypes and demonstrate the value that older employees bring

to the table. Additionally, NLP can empower displaced workers to explore new career paths and re-enter the workforce with confidence, knowing that they have the tools and resources to succeed in a rapidly changing job market. In conclusion, ageism in the workplace is a significant challenge for older workforce employees and displaced workers, but NLP offers a promising solution. By harnessing the power of NLP technology, older workers can enhance their productivity and efficiency, combat ageist stereotypes, and prove their value to employers. Displaced workers can leverage NLP to pivot their careers, identify new opportunities, and showcase their transferable skills to prospective employers. Ultimately, NLP has the potential to empower older and displaced employees to thrive in the workforce and achieve their professional goals.

Job Displacement and Career Pivoting

Job displacement can be a challenging experience for older workforce employees and displaced workers. The uncertainty of not knowing where to turn next can be overwhelming. However, with the rise of technology and advancements in fields such as Natural Language Processing (NLP), there are now more opportunities than ever for older or displaced employees to pivot their careers and find new pathways to success. This subchapter will explore how NLP can benefit older workers and provide a guide for displaced employees looking to pivot their careers.

Natural Language Processing (NLP) is a field of artificial intelligence that focuses on the interaction between computers and human language. It allows computers to understand, interpret, and generate human language, making it an ideal tool for older or displaced employees who may not have traditional technical skills. NLP can help older workers transition into new roles by leveraging their existing knowledge and experience in a way that is relevant to today's digital economy.

For displaced employees looking to pivot their careers, NLP offers a unique opportunity to explore new pathways and industries. By learning how to analyze and process large amounts of text data, individuals can develop skills that are in high demand across a variety of fields, such as marketing, healthcare, and finance. NLP can also help displaced employees identify transferable skills and highlight their unique strengths to potential employers. One of the key benefits of NLP for older or displaced employees is its flexibility and accessibility. Many NLP tools and resources are available online for free or at a low cost, making it easy for individuals to learn at their own pace and on their own schedule. Additionally, NLP can be applied to a wide range of industries and job roles, allowing older workers and displaced employees to explore new career paths that align with their interests and goals. In conclusion, Natural Language Processing (NLP) is a valuable tool for older workforce employees and displaced workers looking to pivot their careers. By leveraging the power of NLP, individuals can tap into new opportunities, develop in-demand skills, and find success in today's rapidly changing job market. Whether you are looking to transition into a new role or explore a different industry, NLP can provide the guidance and support you need to thrive in your career.

Skills Gap and Technology Advancements

In today's rapidly evolving job market, the skills gap continues to widen as technology advancements reshape the way we work. This gap poses a challenge for older workforce employees and displaced workers who may struggle to keep up with the latest trends and tools in their industries. However, there is hope on the horizon in the form of Natural Language Processing (NLP), a cutting-edge technology that can benefit older workers looking to enhance their skill set and pivot their careers.
NLP is a branch of artificial intelligence that focuses on the interaction between computers and human language. It has a wide range of applications, from speech recognition to language translation, making it an invaluable tool for businesses across various industries. For older employees who may feel overwhelmed by the rapid pace of technological change, NLP offers a user-

friendly and intuitive interface that can help bridge the gap between their existing skills and the demands of the modern workplace.

For displaced workers looking to pivot their careers, NLP presents a unique opportunity to transition into a new field without having to start from scratch. By leveraging their existing knowledge and experience, these individuals can quickly upskill and adapt to the demands of a new industry. Whether they are looking to enter the tech sector or explore opportunities in data analysis, NLP can provide the necessary tools and resources to make a successful career transition.

One of the key advantages of NLP is its ability to process and analyze large amounts of unstructured data quickly and accurately. This can be especially beneficial for older workers who may have years of experience but lack the technical skills needed to work with big data. By utilizing NLP tools and techniques, these individuals can leverage their domain expertise to make informed decisions and drive business outcomes.

Overall, the combination of NLP technology and the experience of older workers and displaced employees creates a powerful synergy that can drive innovation and growth in the modern workplace. By embracing this technology and investing in their own professional development, older workers can stay relevant and competitive in today's job market. With the right support and resources, they can leverage the power of NLP to unlock new opportunities and achieve success in their careers.

Chapter 3: Benefits of Natural Language Processing for Older Workers

Enhancing Communication and Collaboration

In today's fast-paced and technology-driven world, effective communication and collaboration are more important than ever. For older workforce employees and displaced workers, mastering these skills can be a key factor in staying relevant and competitive in the job market. Fortunately, Natural Language Processing (NLP) offers a powerful tool for enhancing communication and collaboration in the workplace.

NLP is perfect for older or displaced employees because it takes advantage of the natural language skills that many older workers have honed over years of experience. By using NLP technology, employees can improve their ability to communicate clearly and effectively with colleagues, clients, and customers. NLP can also help older workers adapt to new communication technologies and tools, making it easier for them to collaborate with younger colleagues who may be more comfortable with digital communication platforms. Use your extensive dataset. Your vast knowledge in that brain of yours. Put it to work. learn the skillset and enjoy this new technology Artificial Intelligence.

For displaced employees looking to pivot their careers, NLP can be a game-changer. By learning how to use NLP tools and techniques, displaced workers can enhance their communication and collaboration skills in a variety of industries and roles. NLP can help displaced workers break down communication barriers, navigate complex information, and collaborate with colleagues in different locations or time zones. With NLP, displaced workers can reposition themselves for success in new and emerging fields, such as artificial intelligence, data analysis, or digital marketing. You will find the Nitch that is right for you.

One of the key benefits of NLP for older and displaced workers is its ability to streamline communication processes and improve productivity. By using NLP tools to automate routine tasks, older workers can free up time to focus on more strategic and creative aspects of their work. Displaced workers can also use NLP to enhance their productivity by organizing and prioritizing information more effectively, making it easier to collaborate with team members and meet project deadlines. In this way, NLP can help older and displaced employees stay competitive in a rapidly changing job market.

In conclusion, NLP offers a wealth of opportunities for older and displaced workers looking to enhance their communication and collaboration skills. It has allowed an old dirty contractor the ability to create applications that have the potential to disrupt the way things are currently done. You will hear that word "disrupt" a great deal. By mastering NLP tools and techniques, employees can improve their ability to communicate effectively, collaborate with colleagues, and adapt to new technologies and working environments. With NLP, older and displaced workers can position themselves for success in a variety of industries and roles, ensuring that they remain valuable and competitive members of the workforce for years to come.

Improving Productivity and Efficiency

In today's rapidly evolving workforce, older employees and displaced workers often face challenges when it comes to staying competitive and relevant in their careers. However, there is a powerful tool that can help these individuals not only survive but thrive in the modern workplace: Natural Language Processing (NLP). This subchapter will explore how NLP can significantly improve productivity and efficiency for older workers and displaced employees, making it the perfect solution for those looking to enhance their skills and transition into new roles.

One of the key benefits of NLP for older or displaced employees is its ability to streamline tasks and automate processes. By utilizing NLP technology, individuals can save time and energy on repetitive and time-consuming tasks, allowing them to focus on more strategic and high-value work. This can help older workers stay productive and efficient in their roles, while also enabling displaced employees to adapt quickly to new job requirements and responsibilities.

Moreover, NLP can also help older and displaced workers enhance their communication skills and collaborate more effectively with colleagues. Through NLP-powered tools such as chatbots and virtual assistants, individuals can improve their written and verbal communication skills, making it easier to communicate with team members, clients, and stakeholders. This can lead to better relationships and increased productivity in the workplace, benefiting both the individual and the organization as a whole.

For displaced employees looking to pivot their careers, NLP can be a game-changer. By acquiring new skills in NLP, individuals can open up new opportunities in fields such as data analysis, customer service, and content creation. NLP can help displaced employees retool their skillset and transition into thriving industries that are in high demand, providing them with a pathway to success and job security in the future.

In conclusion, Natural Language Processing is a valuable resource for older workforce employees and displaced workers looking to improve their productivity and efficiency in the modern workplace. By leveraging the power of NLP, individuals can automate tasks, enhance communication skills, and pivot their careers towards new and exciting opportunities. With the right training and support, older and displaced workers can harness the power of NLP to empower themselves and thrive in the ever-changing world of work.

Facilitating Learning and Development

Facilitating learning and development is essential for older workforce employees and displaced workers to remain competitive in today's rapidly changing job market. Natural Language Processing (NLP) offers a unique opportunity for these individuals to enhance their skills and adapt to new technologies. By understanding the benefits of NLP and how it can be used to empower experienced workers, individuals can take control of their career paths and thrive in the digital age.

For older or displaced employees, NLP provides a user-friendly platform that is accessible and easy to use. This technology allows individuals to analyze large amounts of text data quickly and efficiently, making it ideal for those looking to streamline their work processes and stay up-to-date with industry trends. By learning how to harness the power of NLP, older workers can improve their productivity and effectiveness, ultimately leading to greater job satisfaction and career success.

Displaced workers looking to pivot their careers can also benefit from incorporating NLP into their skill set. This technology can help individuals identify new opportunities and trends in various industries, allowing them to pivot their skills and expertise in a meaningful way. By leveraging NLP tools and techniques, displaced workers can explore new career paths, enhance their marketability, and position themselves for success in a competitive job market. NLP is particularly well-suited for older or displaced employees because it does not require extensive technical knowledge or programming skills to use effectively. With user-friendly interfaces and intuitive features, individuals can easily navigate NLP platforms and start incorporating these tools into their daily workflows. By investing time and effort into learning how to use NLP, older workers and displaced employees can unlock new opportunities for growth and development in their careers.

In conclusion, facilitating learning and development through NLP is a valuable resource for older workforce employees and displaced workers looking to thrive in today's digital economy. By embracing this technology and incorporating it into their skill set, individuals can enhance their productivity, adapt to new technologies, and position themselves for success in an ever-changing job market. With the right mindset and commitment to lifelong learning, older workers and displaced employees can empower themselves to achieve their career goals and remain competitive in their fields.

Chapter 4: NLP Tools and Technologies for Career Pivoting

Resume Parsing and Job Matching

Resume parsing and job matching are essential tools in today's competitive job market, especially for older workforce employees and displaced workers. As technology continues to advance, the job search process has become more digitized, making it crucial for individuals to understand how to effectively utilize tools like natural language processing (NLP) to enhance their job search efforts.

For older workforce employees, NLP can be particularly beneficial due to its ability to analyze and interpret large amounts of text data quickly and efficiently. This can help older workers who may have more extensive work experience and skills showcase their qualifications in a way that is easily understandable to potential employers. By using NLP tools for resume parsing, older employees can ensure that their resumes are optimized for applicant tracking systems, increasing their chances of landing interviews.

Displaced workers looking to pivot their careers can also benefit greatly from utilizing NLP tools for job matching. Whether you are looking to transition to a new industry or role, NLP can help you identify transferable skills and relevant job opportunities that align with your career goals. By inputting keywords related to your skills and experiences, NLP algorithms can scan job postings and recommend positions that match your qualifications, making the job search process more targeted and efficient.

One of the key advantages of NLP for displaced employees is its ability to bridge the gap between their current skills and the requirements of new job opportunities. By analyzing job descriptions and identifying common themes and keywords, NLP can help displaced workers understand what skills are in demand in their desired industry and where they may need to upskill or reskill to remain competitive in the job market. This can be especially valuable for older workers who may be looking to transition to a new field or industry.

In conclusion, resume parsing and job matching powered by natural language processing can be powerful tools for older workforce employees and displaced workers looking to navigate the modern job market. By leveraging NLP technology, individuals can optimize their resumes, identify relevant job opportunities, and make informed decisions about their career paths. As technology continues to evolve, it is essential for older and displaced workers to embrace tools like NLP to stay competitive and empower themselves in the job search process.

Skill Assessment and Training Recommendations

As older workforce employees and displaced workers navigate the ever-changing job market, it is essential to assess their current skill set and identify areas for growth and development. One field that holds great promise for individuals in these situations is Natural Language Processing (NLP). NLP is the technology that enables computers to understand, interpret, and generate human language. This subchapter will explore why NLP is perfect for older or displaced employees looking to upskill and pivot their careers.

For older workforce employees who may be looking to transition into a new field or update their skills, NLP offers a range of opportunities. With the rise of artificial intelligence and automation, NLP skills are in high demand across industries such as healthcare, finance, and customer service. By undergoing a skill assessment to identify their strengths and areas for improvement, older workers can tailor their training to focus on NLP techniques and applications that align with their career goals.

Displaced workers who are seeking to pivot their careers in response to job loss or industry shifts can also benefit from exploring NLP as a potential avenue for reemployment. NLP skills are transferable across industries and can open up new opportunities in fields such as data analysis, market research, and content creation. By taking an NLP training course or certification program, displaced workers can enhance their marketability and position themselves for success in a competitive job market.

To effectively transition into a career in NLP, older workforce employees and displaced workers should consider enrolling in training programs that offer hands-on experience with NLP tools and technology. These programs can provide practical skills that can be applied in real-world scenarios, helping individuals gain confidence and proficiency in NLP techniques. Additionally, networking with professionals in the NLP field and seeking mentorship opportunities can further support career growth and development in this rapidly evolving industry.

In conclusion, skill assessment and training recommendations are crucial for older workforce employees and displaced workers looking to empower themselves and thrive in today's job market. By considering the benefits of Natural Language Processing and exploring training opportunities in this field, individuals can position themselves for success and adapt to the changing demands of the workforce. With the right skills and training, older workers and displaced employees can unlock new opportunities and achieve their career goals in the dynamic world of NLP.

Personalized Career Path Suggestions

As older workforce employees and displaced workers navigate the ever-changing landscape of the job market, it can be challenging to determine the best career path moving forward. Fortunately, natural language processing (NLP) offers a unique opportunity for individuals in these situations to explore new career possibilities and find a path that aligns with their skills and interests.

For older or displaced employees looking to transition into a new career, NLP can be particularly beneficial. This technology uses machine learning algorithms to analyze and interpret human language, making it easier to identify trends, patterns, and insights in vast amounts of data. This can be especially useful for individuals who may have years of experience in a particular field but are looking to pivot their careers and explore new opportunities.

One personalized career path suggestion for older workers interested in leveraging NLP is to consider roles in data analysis or data science. With their wealth of experience and knowledge, older employees can bring a unique perspective to these roles and use NLP to extract valuable insights from complex data sets. This can help them make informed decisions and drive business growth in a variety of industries.

For displaced employees looking to pivot their careers, NLP offers a wide range of possibilities. From roles in content creation and marketing to customer service and sales, there are numerous opportunities to leverage NLP skills in a new career path. By honing their skills in natural language processing, displaced workers can position themselves as valuable assets in today's data-driven job market.

In conclusion, personalized career path suggestions for older and displaced workers interested in leveraging NLP can open up a world of possibilities. By exploring roles in data analysis, content creation, marketing, and more, individuals can find new and exciting career opportunities that align with their skills and interests. With the right training and support, older workers and displaced employees can harness the power of natural language processing to empower themselves and thrive in the modern workforce.

Chapter 5: Success Stories of Older Workers Using NLP

Case Study: John Smith, a 55-year-old Sales Manager

In this case study, we will be examining the story of John Smith, a 55-year-old Sales Manager who found himself facing the challenges of a changing workforce. John had been working in sales for over 30 years and had built a successful career for himself. However, as the industry evolved and technology advanced, he began to feel like he was falling behind. He knew he needed to adapt in order to stay relevant in the workforce and continue to excel in his career.

John decided to explore the world of Natural Language Processing (NLP) as a way to enhance his skills and stay competitive in the job market. NLP is a branch of artificial intelligence that focuses on the interaction between computers and humans using natural language. It can be used to analyze and interpret large amounts of text data, making it a valuable tool for businesses looking to gain insights from their customer interactions.

As John delved into the world of NLP, he quickly realized the benefits it could offer him as an older worker. NLP is a field that values experience and expertise, making it a perfect fit for someone like John who has years of industry knowledge under his belt. By leveraging NLP tools and techniques, John was able to streamline his sales processes, improve customer relationships, and stay ahead of the competition.

For older workers like John who may be feeling uncertain about their future in the workforce, NLP offers a way to pivot their careers and explore new opportunities. With the right training and guidance, older workers can use NLP to retrain themselves in a new field, such as data analysis or customer insights. By embracing NLP, older workers can position themselves as valuable assets in the job market and continue to thrive in their careers.

In conclusion, John Smith's case study serves as a powerful example of how older workers and displaced employees can benefit from integrating NLP into their skill set. By embracing new technologies and adapting to the changing landscape of the workforce, older workers can stay competitive, relevant, and empowered in their careers. NLP offers a unique opportunity for older workers to pivot their careers, enhance their skills, and continue to excel in the workforce for years to come.

Case Study: Mary Johnson, a 60-year-old Administrative Assistant

In this case study, we will examine the story of Mary Johnson, a 60-year-old administrative assistant who found herself facing the prospect of displacement in her career. Like many older workers, Mary was concerned about her future in the workforce and unsure of how to navigate the changing landscape of technology and industry. However, with the help of natural language processing (NLP), Mary was able to empower herself and find new opportunities for growth and success.

Mary had been working as an administrative assistant for over 30 years, and she was comfortable in her role. However, when her company announced layoffs due to restructuring, Mary realized that she needed to adapt and find new ways to stay relevant in the workforce. She decided to explore the potential of NLP, a technology that uses artificial intelligence to analyze and understand human language, to help her pivot her career in a new direction. With the assistance of NLP tools and resources, Mary was able to identify her transferable skills and strengths and apply them to new opportunities within her industry. She learned how to use NLP algorithms to analyze job postings and identify the key skills and qualifications that employers were looking for. This allowed her to tailor her resume and cover letter to highlight her relevant experience and increase her chances of landing interviews.

Through the power of NLP, Mary was able to secure a new position as a project coordinator for a technology company. She found that her experience as an administrative assistant gave her a unique perspective and set of skills that were highly valued in her new role. By embracing NLP and leveraging its capabilities, Mary was able to overcome the challenges of displacement and find a fulfilling and rewarding career path that aligned with her interests and strengths.

Mary's story serves as a powerful example of how NLP can benefit older workers and displaced employees looking to pivot their careers. By embracing this technology and leveraging its capabilities, individuals like Mary can empower themselves to navigate the changing landscape of the workforce and find new opportunities for growth and success. As the workforce continues to evolve, NLP offers a valuable tool for older workers and displaced employees to stay competitive, relevant, and empowered in their careers.

Case Study: Robert Brown, a 58-year-old IT Professional

Robert Brown is a 58-year-old IT professional who found himself facing unexpected challenges in the rapidly evolving tech industry. After being laid off from his long-time job due to company downsizing, Robert was unsure of what his next career move should be. Feeling disheartened and discouraged, he began to explore his options for re-entering the workforce as an older worker. As Robert researched different career paths, he came across the field of Natural Language Processing (NLP). Intrigued by the possibilities that NLP offered, he decided to delve deeper into the world of artificial intelligence and machine learning. Through online courses and networking opportunities, Robert gained valuable knowledge and skills that allowed him to pivot his career in a new and exciting direction.

One of the key reasons why NLP was the perfect fit for Robert as an older worker was its focus on language and communication. With decades of experience in the IT industry, Robert possessed a wealth of knowledge that he could apply to the field of NLP. His background in programming and software development gave him a unique advantage in understanding complex algorithms and data structures, making it easier for him to grasp the concepts of NLP.

As Robert continued to expand his skill set in NLP, he found that his experience as an older worker was an asset rather than a liability. His ability to approach problems with a critical and analytical mindset, coupled with his strong work ethic and attention to detail, set him apart from younger professionals in the field. Robert's dedication to continuous learning and growth allowed him to thrive in his new career path and make valuable contributions to his team.

In conclusion, Robert Brown's case study serves as a powerful example of how older workers and displaced employees can benefit from embracing Natural Language Processing as a career opportunity. By leveraging their experience, skills, and knowledge, individuals like Robert can pivot their careers and find success in a rapidly changing job market. Through dedication, perseverance, and a willingness to learn, older workers can empower themselves to thrive in the digital age and contribute meaningfully to the workforce.

These case studies are so similar to my own. My skills in Environmental, Safety and Health, Regulatory Compliance, Project Management, and Facility Management enabled me to draw upon this knowledge I accumulated over the years. I put it to work for myself. I chose to create my own security. I wanted the freedom that Development Operations could provide at my ripe old age. I had to learn much more to create useful and viable applications. I am still learning. The great news is I love it! More on this topic soon.

Chapter 6: Overcoming Barriers and Embracing Change

Addressing Fear of Technology

Many older employees and displaced workers, ME INCLUDED, may experience or did experience a fear of technology, especially when it comes to newer advancements like Natural Language Processing (NLP). It is important to address this fear and show how NLP can benefit older workers and those looking to pivot their careers. By understanding the potential of NLP and how it can be easily integrated into various industries, individuals can overcome their apprehension and embrace this powerful tool. Once it clicks, you will understand just how powerful it is. You will have a new outlook on your newly acquired skills. It will be like the proverbial light switch turning on. It is at this point; you will want to learn as much as possible going forward. When I show my adult Children a new application, they are in awe! My Grandchildren, that's the priceless reaction! To quote my grandson, Paw Paw, you're standing on Business! Now for a 61-year-old grandfather of 7, I have to admit I do not know what that means. However, I suspect it is a pretty decent compliment! The validation from my family serves as the measuring stick of the potential applications success. I have a very diverse family!

One reason why NLP is perfect for older or displaced employees is its user-friendly interface. Unlike other complex technologies, NLP is designed to be intuitive and easy to use, making it accessible to individuals of all ages and backgrounds. With minimal training, you can quickly learn how to leverage NLP to improve their productivity and efficiency in the workplace. This simplicity helps to alleviate the fear of technology and empowers individuals to embrace new tools that can enhance their skills and abilities.

For employees looking to pivot their careers, NLP offers a unique opportunity to explore new avenues and industries. By learning how to use NLP effectively, individuals can expand their skill set and open up new possibilities for employment. Whether it's in customer service, marketing, or data analysis, NLP can be applied in a variety of fields, allowing displaced workers to transition into roles that align with their interests and expertise. This versatility makes NLP a valuable asset for those seeking to adapt to the changing job market.

Furthermore, NLP can help employees stay competitive in today's rapidly evolving workforce. By embracing technology like NLP, individuals can demonstrate their willingness to learn and adapt to new technologies, showcasing their value to employers. This proactive approach not only boosts confidence but also increases job prospects and opportunities for career advancement. By addressing their fear of technology and embracing tools like NLP, individuals can position themselves for success in the digital age.

In conclusion, addressing the fear of technology is crucial for older workers and displaced employees looking to thrive in today's workforce. By understanding the benefits of NLP and how it can empower individuals to excel in their careers, individuals can overcome their apprehension and embrace new technologies with confidence. With its user-friendly interface, versatility, and potential for career advancement, NLP is the perfect tool for older workers and displaced employees to enhance their skills, pivot their careers, and stay competitive in the ever-changing job market.

Building Confidence and Resilience

It's important to focus on building confidence and resilience in order to navigate the ever-changing landscape of the job market. One way to do this is by leveraging the power of Natural Language Processing (NLP), a technology that can benefit older workers in unique ways. By understanding the capabilities of NLP and how it can be applied to various industries, older workers can gain the confidence they need to thrive in today's digital world. Many older or displaced employees may feel overwhelmed by the rapid advancements in technology and the increasing demand for digital skills. However, NLP offers a solution that is accessible and user-friendly for individuals of all ages. By learning how to use NLP tools and software, older workers can enhance their communication skills, analyze data more effectively, and improve their overall productivity. This newfound confidence can help older workers feel more empowered and capable of taking on new challenges in the workforce.

For displaced employees looking to pivot their careers, NLP can be a game-changer. By acquiring skills in NLP, displaced workers can explore new career opportunities in industries such as data analysis, customer service, and marketing. NLP can help displaced workers stand out from the competition by demonstrating their ability to adapt to new technologies and trends. By embracing NLP, displaced workers can boost their confidence and resilience as they navigate the job market and pursue new career paths.

In addition to building confidence and resilience, NLP can also help older workers and displaced employees stay relevant in an increasingly competitive job market. By incorporating NLP into their skill set, older workers can demonstrate their willingness to adapt to new technologies and embrace lifelong learning. This proactive approach can make older workers more attractive to employers and increase their chances of securing fulfilling job opportunities. By investing in NLP training and education, older workers can future-proof their careers and remain competitive in the workforce.

In conclusion, building confidence and resilience is essential for older workforce employees and displaced workers in today's fast-paced job market. By embracing the power of NLP and learning how to leverage its capabilities, older workers can enhance their communication skills, analyze data more effectively, and explore new career opportunities. NLP can help older workers and displaced employees stay relevant, stand out from the competition, and demonstrate their willingness to adapt to new technologies. By investing in NLP training and education, older workers can empower themselves to thrive in the digital age and secure fulfilling job opportunities.

Seeking Support and Mentorship

As older workforce employees and displaced workers, seeking support and mentorship can be crucial in navigating the ever-changing landscape of the job market. In this subchapter, we will explore the importance of seeking out support and mentorship, especially when considering a career transition or advancement in the field of Natural Language Processing (NLP).

Natural Language Processing is a field that involves the interaction between computers and human language. It is a rapidly growing field that offers numerous opportunities for older or displaced employees looking to pivot their careers. By leveraging the power of NLP, individuals can enhance their skills and remain competitive in the job market. Seeking support and mentorship from experienced professionals in the field can help older workers navigate the complexities of NLP and stay ahead of the curve.

For displaced employees looking to pivot their careers, NLP can offer a fresh start and new opportunities for growth. By connecting with mentors who have experience in NLP, displaced workers can gain valuable insights and guidance on how to transition into this field. Mentors can provide advice on how to develop the necessary skills and knowledge required for a career in NLP, as well as offer support and encouragement throughout the transition process.

In seeking support and mentorship, older workforce employees and displaced workers can benefit from the wisdom and expertise of those who have already paved the way in the field of NLP. Mentors can provide valuable insights on industry trends, best practices, and potential career paths within NLP. By building relationships with mentors, individuals can gain access to valuable resources, networking opportunities, and career development support that can help them succeed in their chosen field.

In conclusion, seeking support and mentorship is essential for older workforce employees and displaced workers looking to leverage the power of Natural Language Processing in their careers. By connecting with experienced professionals in the field, individuals can gain valuable insights, guidance, and encouragement to navigate the complexities of NLP and achieve their career goals. By taking advantage of mentorship opportunities, older workers and displaced employees can position themselves for success and thrive in the competitive job market.

Chapter 7: Future Trends and Opportunities in NLP for Older Workers

The Role of AI in the Future Workplace

In the rapidly evolving landscape of the modern workplace, the role of artificial intelligence (AI) is becoming increasingly prominent. For older workforce employees and displaced workers, understanding and adapting to the integration of AI in the workplace is crucial for maintaining relevance in today's job market. This subchapter will explore the ways in which AI, specifically Natural Language Processing (NLP), can benefit older and displaced workers as they navigate the future of work.

Natural Language Processing, a subset of AI that focuses on the interaction between computers and human language, is particularly well-suited for older or displaced employees. NLP technologies can assist individuals in tasks such as data analysis, customer service, and content creation, making them valuable assets in a variety of industries. For older workers who may be less familiar with the latest technological advancements, NLP provides an accessible entry point into the world of AI, allowing them to leverage their existing skills and experience in new and innovative ways.

For displaced employees looking to pivot their careers in the wake of job loss or industry shifts, NLP offers a versatile toolset for retraining and upskilling. By learning how to utilize NLP technologies, displaced workers can enhance their marketability and competitiveness in a rapidly changing job market. NLP can help individuals transition into new roles or industries by providing them with the skills and capabilities needed to succeed in a digital-first world.

Furthermore, NLP can help older and displaced workers overcome age-related or experience-related biases in the job market. By demonstrating proficiency in NLP technologies, individuals can showcase their adaptability, willingness to learn, and problem-solving abilities, regardless of their age or previous job experience. This can open up new opportunities for older or displaced workers to re-enter the workforce or explore alternative career paths that align with their interests and strengths.

In conclusion, the integration of AI, particularly NLP, in the future workplace presents numerous opportunities for older and displaced workers to thrive in a rapidly changing job market. By embracing NLP technologies and leveraging their unique skills and experiences, older and displaced employees can position themselves for success in a digital-first world. Empowering the experienced with NLP is not only beneficial for individual career growth but also for driving innovation and productivity in the workplace as a whole.

Continuous Learning and Adaptability

Continuous learning and adaptability are key components for success in today's ever-changing workforce. As older workforce employees and displaced workers, it is crucial to stay up to date with the latest technologies and trends in order to remain competitive in the job market. This is true no matter what industry you're in. One area that is particularly well-suited for displaced employees is Natural Language Processing (NLP) that is revolutionizing industries such as healthcare, finance, and customer service.

NLP is artificial intelligence that focuses on the interaction between computers and humans through natural language. It enables machines to understand, interpret, and generate human language, allowing for more efficient communication and decision-making. Older employees and displaced workers can benefit greatly from NLP as it provides opportunities for career advancement and job security in industries that are rapidly adopting this technology.

For displaced employees looking to pivot their careers, NLP offers a unique opportunity to transfer their skills and expertise to a new and growing field. By learning the fundamentals of NLP, displaced workers can position themselves as valuable assets to companies looking to implement this technology into their operations. With the right training and education, older employees and displaced workers can successfully transition into roles that leverage their existing skills while also expanding their knowledge in NLP.

Continuous learning is essential for displaced workers to stay relevant in today's job market. By investing in their education and training in NLP, individuals can open up new opportunities for themselves and secure their future in a rapidly evolving workforce. Additionally, adaptability is key for success in any career, and NLP provides a platform for older employees and displaced workers to showcase their ability to learn and grow in response to changing industry demands.

In conclusion, continuous learning and adaptability are essential for older employees and displaced workers to thrive in today's workforce. NLP presents a unique opportunity for individuals in these groups to upskill and pivot their careers towards a promising and in-demand field. By embracing the opportunities that NLP offers, older employees and displaced workers can position themselves for success in a rapidly changing job market.

Creating a More Inclusive Work Environment

Creating a more inclusive work environment is crucial for the success and well-being of all employees, including older workforce employees and displaced workers. By fostering a more inclusive workplace, organizations can benefit from a diverse range of perspectives and experiences, leading to increased creativity, innovation, and productivity. In this subchapter, we will explore how natural language processing (NLP) can help older and displaced workers thrive in the modern workplace.

Natural language processing, artificial intelligence, focuses on enabling computers to understand, interpret, and generate human language. This technology is particularly well-suited for employees who may be looking to enhance their skills and remain competitive in today's rapidly evolving work environment. NLP tools can help older workers improve their communication skills, analyze large amounts of text data, and automate repetitive tasks, making it easier for them to adapt to new technologies and stay relevant in their careers.

For displaced employees looking to pivot their careers, natural language processing (NLP) offers a unique opportunity to explore new job opportunities and industries. By mastering NLP tools and techniques, displaced workers can leverage their existing skills and experiences to pursue careers in fields such as data analysis, content creation, and customer service. NLP can help displaced employees enhance their resume, stand out to potential employers, and demonstrate their ability to learn and adapt to new technologies.

In order to create a more inclusive work environment for older and displaced workers, organizations must prioritize training and support programs that help employees develop their skills and adapt to new technologies. By investing in NLP training and resources, employers can empower older and displaced workers to succeed in the modern workplace and contribute their unique perspectives and experiences to the organization. Additionally, organizations can create mentorship programs, networking opportunities, and flexible work arrangements to support older and displaced workers as they navigate their career transitions.

In conclusion, creating a more inclusive work environment for older and displaced workers is essential for fostering a diverse and innovative workforce. By leveraging natural language processing (NLP) technology, organizations can empower older and displaced employees to enhance their skills, pivot their careers, and thrive in the modern workplace. By investing in training, support, and mentorship programs, employers can ensure that older and displaced workers have the resources they need to succeed and contribute to the success of the organization.

Chapter 8: Conclusion and Call to Action

Recap of Key Points

In this subchapter, we will recap some of the key points discussed in our book, "Empowering the Experienced: How Natural Language Processing Can Benefit Older Workers." This information is particularly relevant for older workforce employees and displaced workers who are looking to enhance their skills and stay competitive in today's rapidly evolving job market.

First and foremost, we have highlighted the reasons why Natural Language Processing (NLP) is the perfect fit for older or displaced employees. NLP is a branch of artificial intelligence that focuses on enabling computers to understand and generate human language. This technology can be especially advantageous for older workers who may have decades of industry experience but need to update their skills to remain relevant in a digital world.

For displaced employees looking to pivot their careers, NLP offers a unique opportunity to transition into a new field or industry. By learning how to utilize NLP tools and techniques, individuals can enhance their job prospects and open up new opportunities for themselves. NLP can be particularly beneficial for displaced workers who are looking to leverage their existing skills and experience in a different way.

Additionally, we have discussed the various ways in which NLP can be applied in different industries and job roles. From customer service and marketing to healthcare and finance, NLP has the potential to revolutionize how work is done across a wide range of sectors. By familiarizing themselves with NLP technology, older workers and displaced employees can position themselves as valuable assets to employers seeking to innovate and adapt to changing market demands.

In conclusion, "Empowering the Experienced: How Natural Language Processing Can Benefit Older Workers" serves as a valuable resource for older workforce employees and displaced workers who are seeking to stay competitive in today's job market. By understanding the potential of NLP and how it can be leveraged to enhance their skills and career prospects, individuals can empower themselves to succeed in an increasingly digital world. It is never too late to learn and grow, and NLP provides a unique opportunity for older workers and displaced employees to do just that.

Empowering Older Workers with NLP

As older workforce employees and displaced workers navigate the ever-changing landscape of the job market, it is crucial for them to explore new technologies that can help them stay relevant and competitive. One such technology that holds great promise for older workers is Natural Language Processing (NLP). NLP is a branch of artificial intelligence that focuses on the interaction between computers and human language, enabling machines to understand, interpret, and generate human language. This technology can be a game-changer for older workers looking to upgrade their skills and remain valuable in the workforce.

One of the reasons why NLP is perfect for older or displaced employees is its user-friendly nature. NLP tools and applications are designed to be intuitive and easy to use, making it accessible even for those who may not have a strong technical background. This means that older workers can quickly learn how to leverage NLP for tasks such as data analysis, customer service, and content creation without the need for extensive training or re-education. This can give older workers a competitive edge in a job market that increasingly values digital skills.

For displaced employees looking to pivot their careers, NLP can be a valuable tool for exploring new opportunities and industries. By leveraging NLP tools for tasks such as resume parsing, job matching, and skills assessment, displaced workers can identify potential career paths that align with their interests, experiences, and strengths. This can help them transition into new roles and industries more smoothly and confidently, increasing their chances of success in the job market.

Moreover, NLP can also help older workers and displaced employees stay connected and engaged in the digital age. By using NLP-powered communication tools, such as chatbots and virtual assistants, older workers can improve their productivity, efficiency, and collaboration with colleagues and clients. This can help them stay relevant and competitive in a workforce that is increasingly reliant on digital communication and collaboration tools.

In conclusion, NLP has the potential to empower older workers and displaced employees by providing them with the tools and resources they need to thrive in the modern job market. By leveraging NLP technologies for tasks such as data analysis, career exploration, and communication, older workers can enhance their skills, stay connected, and remain valuable assets to their employers. As the workforce continues to evolve, it is essential for older workers to embrace new technologies like NLP to adapt, grow, and succeed in their careers.

Taking the First Steps towards a Brighter Future

Taking the first steps towards a brighter future can be a daunting task, especially for older workforce employees and displaced workers. However, with the advancements in technology, specifically Natural Language Processing (NLP), there are new and exciting opportunities for those looking to enhance their skills and pivot their careers. This subchapter will explore why NLP is perfect for older or displaced employees and how it can benefit those looking to make a change in their professional lives.

One of the reasons why NLP is perfect for older and displaced employees is its user-friendly interface and intuitive design. NLP technology allows individuals to interact with computers and devices using natural language, making it easier for those who may not be as familiar with traditional programming languages. This accessibility opens up a whole new world of possibilities for older workers who may be looking to learn new skills or pivot their careers in a different direction.

NLP offers a unique opportunity to explore new industries and fields. By harnessing the power of NLP, individuals can analyze vast amounts of text data, identify patterns and trends, and make data-driven decisions. This can be especially beneficial for those looking to transition into roles that require strong analytical and problem-solving skills, such as data analysis or business intelligence.

Additionally, NLP technology can help employees stay competitive in today's rapidly changing job market. By learning how to use NLP tools and techniques, individuals can enhance their skill set, make themselves more marketable to potential employers, and increase their chances of finding fulfilling and rewarding work. This can be a game-changer for those who may be struggling to find their place in the workforce or who are looking to reinvent themselves later in their careers.

In conclusion, taking the first steps towards a brighter future with NLP technology can be a game-changer for older or displaced employees. By leveraging the power of NLP, individuals can enhance their skills, explore new career opportunities, and stay competitive in today's job market. Whether you're looking to learn something new, pivot your career, or reinvent yourself later in life, NLP technology can help you achieve your goals and empower you to take control of your professional future. Your journey starts with the first step. Take it today! Do something positive for yourself!

www.ingramcontent.com/pod-product-compliance
Lightning Source LLC
Chambersburg PA
CBHW031515210526
45464CB00007B/2921